Katrin Hanses

Concrete
Construction

Katrin Hanses

Concrete
Construction

BIRKHÄUSER
BASEL

Contents

Foreword

As a monolithic, cast material with a high loadbearing capacity, concrete is used in many areas of building. When combined with reinforcement steel in the form of reinforced concrete the material can bridge large spans and is very durable. Surfaces that differ in terms of structure and colour can be produced using different formwork elements and admixtures. A good knowledge of this material, its properties and the process by which it is made is indispensable for the architect's creative process.

Reinforced concrete has been tried and tested over a long period and is widely used in both architecture and civil engineering. Generations of architects have discovered ever new and creative ways of using the material. In recent years, thanks to innovative reinforcement elements and processing methods, marked progress has been made in building with concrete, so that the diversity of this material has increased substantially, and it has proved possible to develop new areas of use.

It is at this point that this new book *Basics Concrete Construction* begins and gives the reader an understanding of the special qualities of concrete and the constructional possibilities that it offers. From the development of knowledge about the material, to the special production methods of concrete building parts, to the connections between these parts, it gives the architecture student the means for reflecting on creative solutions and developing new approaches to the construction of buildings.

Bert Bielefeld, Editor

Introduction

Concrete is one of the most important materials in architecture and civil engineering. As a poured material it offers a variety of possibilities for architectural design and in making loadbearing building parts. Concrete allows monolithic ways of building – i.e. buildings which are "poured in one cast" and through the use of various additives and composite materials its abilities are extremely varied. The concrete mix has a great influence on the later qualities of the material and can be adapted to meet the individual demands made on the building element. In designing concrete a great deal is possible – from the small to the extremely large scale.

As a material it has a strength that allows it to be used in primary and secondary constructions as prefabricated elements so that, with consistent planning, economic, high-quality execution is possible. When designing concrete buildings various building parts must be fitted together, different means of production combined, and the relationship between the details and the structure of the whole must be resolved. A wide range of knowledge about the fabrication, construction and later treatment is indispensable. To explore the potential and possibilities of the material this basic knowledge about concrete is conveyed here, opening the way for an intensive examination of the material.

Building material

CONSTITUENT MATERIALS

Concrete is traditionally made of water, cement and aggregate. To these can be added air and various additives and admixtures, which are being continuously developed. Consequently, concrete's capacity and the range of areas in which it can be used are growing all the time.

The proportion of water to cement and the consistency of the cement paste produced in this way have a major influence on the quality and workability of the fresh concrete. Mixing causes the concrete to become malleable. The duration of the mixing process is strictly laid down for each kind of concrete mix. The cement paste must surround the aggregate, holding the pieces together and filling any hollows.

In terms of amount, the aggregate plays the major role in concrete, and is most important for the quality of the concrete. A fine-grained aggregate should be chosen particularly for exposed concrete building elements or those on which great demands are made.

Aggregate

The aggregate can consist of broken or unbroken pieces. Natural mineral materials are traditionally used but waste products or byproducts from industry can often also be employed. They need to have a certain grain strength and it must be possible to combine them with the paste so that the durability of the concrete is not impaired.

The aggregate is differentiated according to its origins, structure, unit weight, grain form and grain size. There are also different demands in terms of durability and the geometrical, chemical and physical properties of the grain, as well as with regard to frost resistance. In this respect there are special grain groups, compositions or forms.

Depending on the nature of the particular material, the aggregate must be processed for use in making concrete. The grain size distribution curve (a diagram depicting the composition of grain mixes) is decisive for the quality of the concrete produced. This distribution curve is produced by sieving the aggregate through sieves of different mesh sizes. Standard distribution curves for grain mixes are 8 mm, 16 mm, 32 mm and 63 mm, the maximum grain size, which in certain circumstances must be produced by fragmenting, sieving or washing.

Grain size distribution curve

Up to a grain size of 0.125 mm we are dealing with powder. This fine material has a positive effect on the workability of fresh concrete and ensures a dense structure, which is particularly important for exposed or watertight concrete. However, the higher amount of cement also makes it more expensive to produce.

One of the further main ingredients of concrete is cement, which can be subdivided into five main kinds (CEM I–V). > Tab. 1 Cement is a hydraulic binder that holds the concrete together.

Cement

Tab. 1: Kinds of cement

Kind of cement	Definition
CEM I	Portland cement: strength class 32.5R (high initial strength)
CEM II	Portland composite cement: various main ingredients (slag sand and limestone), strength class 42.5N
CEM III	Blast furnace cement (Portland cement, clinker and slag sand), strength class 32.5N
CEM IV	Pozzolanic cement
CEM V	Composite cement

Blast furnace cement (CEM III) is used for the production of ultra high performance concrete (UHPC). Alongside its low porosity (which protects against ingress of liquid) it has numerous other positive qualities. Less primary energy is required to produce it, and it saves on natural resources. Cracking due to thermal stress is rare and it is more resistant to chemicals and salts.

Water-cement value   What is called the w/c value should be determined at the planning stage in accordance with the appearance required and the particular function. This describes the proportion of water to cement and influences the properties of the concrete. The higher the w/c value, the lower the strength. The proportion of water to cement can also have an effect on the colour: a lower w/c value makes the surface appear darker, whereas a higher value produces a lighter-coloured surface.

In order for concrete to cure (= hydration), it must have a w/c value of at least 0.4 (which represents 40% water). If more water is added the cement can no longer bind the water, and the liquid emerges ("bleeds"). If the proportion of cement is too high there is a danger of too rapid drying and shrinking.

Admixtures   Admixtures can be in liquid or powder form or can also be added as granulate or a paste. They influence the quality of the fresh or solid concrete by chemical or physical processes. For example, they can change workability or air content. > Tab. 2 The admixtures have only a minor effect on the mass

● of the fresh concrete and their volume can therefore be ignored.

Additives   Additives are different materials that are added to concrete to influence or achieve certain properties. A distinction is made between two different groups:

Type I: Almost inactive concrete additives (stone dust, pigment)

Type II: Pozzolanic or latent hydraulic concrete additives (fly ash, silica dust)

Tab. 2: Standard concrete admixtures

Admixtures	Function
Concrete plasticiser and super plasticiser	Gives the concrete a more plastic consistency despite the low water content so that it flows better. This makes it easier to distribute the fresh concrete in the formwork.
Air-entraining agent	Leads to the formation of air bubbles by means of chemical foaming. A higher proportion of air improves concrete's thermal insulation properties.
Sealant	Makes the solid concrete waterproof.
Retardant	Delays the curing of the fresh concrete, important in large building parts that are to be produced without construction joints.
Accelerator	Accelerates the curing and hardening process, is particularly important in sprayed concrete to ensure that it quickly reaches a basic stability and does not drip (for example, when used in building work overhead).
Pressing aids	Improves the flowability. Used primarily in prestressed concrete.
Stabiliser	Prevents "bleeding" (emergence of water) and ensures better cohesion of the mix.

As with aggregate, the additives should be taken into account as part of the volume, according to their properties and the amount added. ■

For the consistency of concrete it is important that throughout the production process no separation of the constituent elements should take place. Consistency is the yardstick for the strength of fresh concrete, which must be flowable enough to allow good workability. Good flowability also stands for good fresh concrete quality; consistency should be determined before the start of construction and should be monitored during production.

Concrete consistency

The compacting technique should be chosen according to consistency. Consistency is divided into flow spread and compaction classes. > Tabs. 3 and 4 These are arrived at by using flow table tests and compaction tests.

● **Example:** A plasticiser based on PCE (polycarboxylate ether) is added to the concrete to improve its flowability when being poured. In addition, through the material itself, air is removed. Later compacting is therefore unnecessary, even in the case of compact geometries or high amounts of reinforcement. A smooth, almost pore-free surface and a very efficient concrete is achieved.

■ **Tip:** Additives can also be used for design purposes. For instance, pigments can be used to colour concrete, translucency can be achieved, or the surface can be given a structure. For coloured areas of concrete it makes sense to test the effect of additives and the amount to be used on sample areas.

Tab. 3: Classes according to flow table spread

Consistency	Class	Flow table spread d	Compacting technique
Stiff concrete	F1	≤ 34 cm	Powerful vibrating or stamping, thin lift fill
Plastic concrete	F2	35–41 cm	Compacting by vibrating
Soft concrete	F3	42–48 cm	Light vibrating or rodding (for high-strength in-situ concrete of at least class F3)
Very soft concrete	F4	49–55 cm	Rodding, is produced using plasticiser
Flowable concrete	F5	56–62 cm	Rodding, is produced using plasticiser
Very flowable concrete	F6	≥ 63 cm	Only by gravity, plasticiser
Self-compacting concrete	SVB		Compacted only by gravity, air is removed, flows well between reinforcement, particularly suitable for exposed concrete

Tab. 4: Classes according to compaction

Consistency	Class	Compaction c
Very stiff concrete	C0	≥ 1.46
Stiff concrete	C1	1.45–1.26
Sculptural concrete	C2	1.25–1.11
Soft concrete	C3	1.10–1.04

KINDS OF CONCRETE

Distinctions are drawn between different kinds of concrete based on the composition, additives, surfaces, production process, or the nature of the reinforcement > Tabs. 5 and 6 This always affects the planning and design of a building made of (reinforced) concrete. For example, building parts must be produced or maintained differently depending on the kind of concrete used.

There are a wide variety of different types of concrete. They are differentiated according to several criteria:

— Unit weight
— Compressive strength
— Application
— Special properties

The compressive strength of concrete is given in what are called strength classes, which begin with C for "concrete" (lightweight concrete = LC). This is followed by two numbers that are determined by test processes (cylinder strength/cube crushing strength). The greater the strength, the greater the difference between cylinder and cube. A low strength class also means a low w/c value. > Chapter Building material, Constituent materials

Tab. 5: Kinds of concrete according to unit weight and strength

Kind of concrete	Dry unit weight	Strength classes
Lightweight concrete	< 2000 kg/m^3 (theoretically possible from 350 kg/m^3)	LC 8/9 to LC 50/55 (LC 55/60 to LC 80/88 = high-strength lightweight concrete)
Normal concrete	2000–2600 kg/m^3	C8/10 to C50/60 C55/67 to C80/95 = high-strength concrete (C90/105 and C100/115 in particular cases)
Heavy concrete	2600–5900 kg/m^3	C8/10 to C50/60 C55/67 to C80/95 = high-strength concrete (C90/105 and C100/115 in particular cases)

Tab. 6: Kinds of concrete

Kind of concrete	Described according to	Definition
Normal concrete	Reference point for all others	Generally used concrete
Lightweight concrete	Concrete mix	By adding coarse light aggregate (expanded clay aggregate), better insulating properties are achieved. Lower strength but also lower weight.
Aerated concrete	Concrete mix	A kind of lightweight concrete. Instead of aggregate, aerated concrete contains air bubbles, which are produced through a chemical process and further improve the insulating qualities.
Heavy concrete	Concrete mix/strength class	Particularly heavy aggregate (e.g. barite, iron ore, steel granulate etc.) with high dry unit weight, used above all for protection against radiation or similar.
Ultra high performance concrete (UHPC)	Concrete mix/strength class	Uses furnace cement instead of Portland cement, very high strength and good durability, allows slender design, saves resources and can be used economically.
Water-impermeable concrete	Concrete mix/properties	Concrete with a high resistance to the entry of water, used above all to seal building parts in the ground (see Chapter Building parts, Footings/foundations)
Waterproof concrete	Concrete mix/properties	Similar to water-impermeable concrete, addition of barriers.
Self-compacting concrete	Concrete mix/additives	Addition of plasticiser, no additional compacting necessary, finely pored surface and complex geometries possible.
Translucent concrete	Concrete mix/additives	Glass optical fibres are introduced into the fine concrete. Depending on their density and arrangement they create particular patterns and enable the concrete to become translucent.
Refractory concrete	Concrete mix/additives	Withstands temperatures from 500 to 2000 °C
Recycled concrete	Concrete mix/additives	Aggregate produced from recycled materials (e.g. building rubble)
Concrete screed	Concrete mix	Small aggregate size to allow thin layers to be made. Especially for making floor layers.

Tab. 6: Kinds of concrete

Prestressed concrete	Structural design/kind of reinforcement	Steel reinforcement is pre-spanned (pre-stretched), creating a high compressive stress. The properties of concrete are better exploited, more efficient building parts are produced. The stiffness prevents major deflection even with large spans.
Textile concrete	Kind of reinforcement	Composite material with low thickness and high resistance to compression and deflection. Flexible forms possible through particular reinforcing materials.
Fibre concrete	Kind of reinforcement	Fibres can be made of plastic, glass fibre, carbon, natural fibres or similar.
Self-cleaning concrete	Surface characteristic	The surface is treated with photocatalytically effective metal oxides or sulphides. The self-cleansing, pollutant disintegrating effect is achieved by light. In addition, the surface must by super-hydrophobe (water repellent) or super-hydrophile (water-attractive).
Exposed (fair-faced) concrete	Surface characteristic	Smooth, fine-pored surface, generally produced as a prefabricated part.
Tamped or compressed concrete	Concreting process	Unreinforced, historic method of use, produced layer by layer, compacted by tamping. High density, hardly any shrinking, few cracks.
Spun concrete	Concreting process	For tubes, piles or masts, compacted by a rapidly rotating steel formwork, low w/c value, very solid, dense concrete (up to C100/115). Hollow cross sections are created that can also be used to take service runs.
Sprayed concrete	Concreting process	Is particularly flowable and hardens quickly. Applied through a spray nozzle using pressurised air. This method allows concrete that is already compacted to be applied to a wide area.
Vacuum concrete	Concreting process	Introduction of the fresh concrete by means of a vacuum. At the same time superfluous water is suctioned off and a dense surface with few cracks is created.

REINFORCEMENT

Concrete is a freely formable building material and is used in combination with very different materials. Most often it is used as part of a composite construction together with steel, and is known then as "reinforced concrete". As with every composite construction, the materials that make up reinforced concrete are used in accordance with their specific properties.

Concrete is characterised by a high compressive strength, while steel can handle high tensile forces. Together they form a highly efficient material that can handle heavy loads and bridge considerable spans. At the same time the combination of these two materials balances out their potential weaknesses. Steel tends to rust (corrode) but when completely covered by concrete it is protected from this process.

Fig. 1: Reinforcement steel   Fig. 2: Spacer made of plastic

However, the easy formability of concrete is restricted by the use of
steel reinforcement. This rigid material generally dictates an orthogonal
way of building, determined by financial and material budgets.

Steel is the main kind of concrete reinforcement in building above
and below ground level. However, more recently other kinds of reinforcement, such as glass or carbon fibres, have become established. They are
pioneering trends and offer new design possibilities for both surfaces
and forms.

Steel reinforcement is measured and dimensioned on the basis of
the forces expected. Reinforced concrete building parts can also be made
under a certain mechanical prestressing, which enables them to be used
in an even more effective and efficient way.

The reinforcement in concrete allows homogeneous, solid connections to be made to other building parts and thus contributes to the monolithic building method. Steel is particularly suitable as reinforcement
because concrete and steel have similar thermal expansion behaviour
and thus during the changing climatic conditions over the course of a
year no internal tensions are produced in the building part.

Various methods have proved effective in introducing steel into concrete. Reinforcement baskets, mats and rods are used in orthogonal
building parts. They are fixed according to the reinforcement plan, which
is based on the structural engineer's calculations and dimensioning.

The surface of the steel is usually ribbed or structured in some way
to create a better bind with the concrete. This allows a direct transfer of
forces to the concrete. > Fig. 1

To ensure that the reinforcement remains in position when the
concrete is being poured it is fixed using spacers. > Fig. 2 These spacers
primarily ensure the necessary concrete cover. They can be made of
various materials, such as fibre concrete, cast concrete, plastic or
steel.

Steel reinforcement

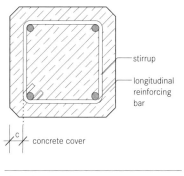

stirrup

longitudinal
reinforcing
bar

c

concrete cover

Fig. 3: Concrete cover

Concrete cover

Concrete cover means the distance between the outer surface of the concrete and the outermost layer of reinforcement in the concrete. > Fig. 3 Concrete cover does not have a structural function; its purpose is to prevent damage occurring to the building part. It ensures that the concrete encases the steel on all sides so that it is not exposed to the external air. If the cover is insufficient the concrete can flake off. The steel is then no longer covered and may corrode. The building part is damaged fundamentally in the long term and this can lead to failure. Cover should not be less than 15 mm, and is generally between 20 and 25 mm.

The concrete cover also ensures fire safety, as the concrete keeps the heat away from the sensitive steel. As with the outside cover, a distance must be kept within the building part between the steel bars. This distance must be at least 2 cm, and it should never be less than the diameter of the largest bar. Depending on the aggregate size, even greater distances may be necessary. If an internal vibrator is to be used to compact the concrete, sufficiently large gaps must be provided.

Spalling

If concrete carbonates in the course of time, moisture, CO_2 and acid solutions can be absorbed. The reinforcement begins to corrode, increasing in volume in the process. The expansion causes the concrete cover to flake off (= spalling), exposing the reinforcement.

Corrosion

Corrosion is the term used to describe the rusting of steel reinforcement. The hardening (hydration) of cement produces calcium hydroxide, which is responsible for the alkaline milieu in concrete. The alkalinity in concrete protects the steel against corrosion. Both the pH of the concrete and the concrete cover are of fundamental importance in ensuring that a reinforced concrete building part functions properly.

Corrosion can be divided into two kinds depending on whether it is caused by carbonation or by the entry of chlorides. > Tab. 7 The demands made on a building part define its exposure class, which lays down the minimum cement content, the highest permissible water-cement value, and any post-treatment of the concrete.

Tab. 7: Exposure classes for reinforcement corrosion

	Class	Description of the surroundings	Examples
Corrosion of the reinforcement due to carbonation	XC1	Dry or constantly wet	Building parts in interior spaces, normal air humidity; building parts that are constantly under water
	XC2	Wet, rarely dry	Parts of water tanks; foundations
	XC3	Moderately damp	Open halls, interiors with high air humidity, cattle sheds etc.
	XC4	Alternately wet and dry	External building parts directly exposed to rain, buildings in areas between high and low water levels
Reinforcement corrosion caused by chloride	XD1	Moderate damp	Buildings in areas sprayed from traffic surfaces; individual garages
	XD2	Wet, rarely dry	Swimming pools; building parts that are exposed to industrial water containing chloride
	XD3	Alternately wet and dry	Building parts subject to water sprayed from roads treated with de-icing salt; parking decks driven on directly
Reinforcement corrosion caused by chloride from seawater	XS1	Salty air, but no contact with seawater	External building parts near the coast
	XS2	Under water	Parts of buildings in harbours that are constantly under water
	XS3	Areas subject to tides, sprayed water and mist	Quay walls in harbours

Prestressing offers a way to make even better use of the fundamental material properties of steel and concrete. In prestressed concrete the steel reinforcement is prestretched according to precise calculations, creating high compressive stress in the concrete building part. This functions above all through the off-centre position of the reinforcement in the cross section of the building part. When mounting the part, the prestressing means that there are no tensile forces in the concrete. Highly efficient building parts are made with high stiffness and low deflection that can bridge considerable spans. > Fig. 4

Prestressed concrete

○ **Note:** Carbonation = through contact with CO_2 the alkaline milieu in the concrete is neutralised. The pH sinks and the steel is no longer protected from corrosion.

○ **Note:** Alkalinity describes the strength of an alkali. Milieus with a pH above 7 are regarded as alkaline. Cement stone has a pH of ≥ 12, a very high alkalinity.

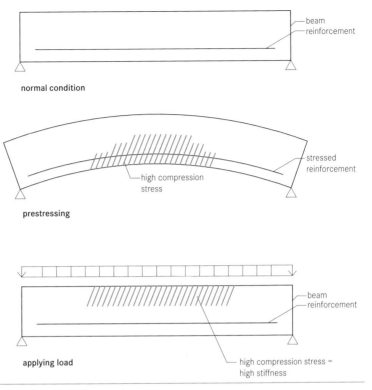

normal condition

high compression
stress

stressed
reinforcement

prestressing

beam
reinforcement

beam
reinforcement

applying load

high compression stress =
high stiffness

Fig. 4: The principle of stressed concrete

Other materials for reinforcement

Alongside steel reinforcement and its further developments, there are also other reinforcing materials that help concrete play its loadbearing role. These are at different stages of development and some of them do not yet have official authorisation. Many can be used as fibre additives, in the form of textiles or mats. > Tab. 8

Fibre concrete

Fibre reinforced concrete is evenly reinforced with fibres that are generally made from steel, plastic or carbon. This kind of reinforcement can be used for different purposes. It improves the tensile strength or also the resistance to impact. In this case, additional steel can sometimes be dispensed with. In conjunction with standard steel reinforcement, fibre reinforcement can be used to ensure less deformation or to minimise the formation of cracks.

In selecting the fibres it is important that the material can be used permanently in the alkaline milieu of the concrete and that it connects with the concrete. Different production processes are used depending

Tab. 8: Reinforcement materials

Material	Characteristic	Use	Innovation phase
Carbon	Very light and tension resistant. Relatively high production costs, but great material savings as almost no concrete cover. Extremely thin building parts are possible.	Fibre or textile	Some already approved. Used principally in improving existing buildings.
Natural fibre	For example, hemp, flax or cellulose; high elasticity, low weight. Cannot be easily distributed in concrete and influence the w/c value.	Fibre	At the testing phase
Glass fibre	Can be used in much the same way as carbon, but less efficient.	Fibre or textile	Ready for the market
Steel fibre	As an alternative or together with normal steel reinforcement	Fibre	Ready for the market
Plastic fibre	Generally made of polypropylene, against micro-cracking in fresh concrete. Used also in high-performance concrete or for fire protection.	Fibre	Ready for the market

upon the fibre type, and they can to some extent be adapted to the flow of forces in the building.

Exactly as with concrete reinforced with steel, the tension forces in textile reinforced concrete are taken up by the reinforcement. The textiles are produced from individual fibres (filaments), which, similarly to fibre concrete, generally consist of glass or carbon. The filaments are woven into yarn and processed to form mats or meshes. The precision with which the reinforcement can be positioned is also the great advantage compared to fibre reinforced concrete: there is no danger of clumps or concentrations forming or of the fibres being unevenly distributed. The textiles can also adapt three-dimensionally to the flow of forces. The filigree material is prefabricated precisely to meet the specific requirements and consequently is utilised in an almost perfect way. The concrete that is used for textile reinforced building parts must be flowable and fine-grain (maximum grain size 1 mm), to ensure that it settles evenly around the textile and in the mesh.

In contrast to steel reinforced concrete, textile concrete is not subject to threat from corrosion and therefore no minimum amounts of cover are required. It is also characterised by its low weight, slender and precise building parts and an accordingly high efficiency. At present it is used in maintenance work or in improving building parts. Production costs are higher than those for steel reinforced concrete.

Textile concrete

MATERIAL PROPERTIES

Thermal insulation   The nature of a building material determines its properties in terms of building physics. The thermal capacities of concrete influence the values of, for instance, the material's density, thermal conductivity and water content. Concrete is the decisive material in the composite reinforced concrete. It has a high density and therefore stores heat well. The solid nature of concrete ensures that this heat is given off after a lapse of time, allowing possible extremes of temperature to be evened out.

Thermal conductivity defines how easily heat is conducted through layers of a building part. Concrete has a high thermal conductivity, which is why the concrete parts of the thermal envelope must be given additional thermal insulation. > Tab. 9 The concrete mix and the additives can also be altered in order to avoid high heat transmission losses. One example of this is aerated concrete, in which a high proportion of air voids ensures a better thermal insulation effect. > Chapter Building material, Kinds of concrete

Sound insulation   Concrete also has good sound insulation properties on account of its high bulk density. The denser and heavier a building material is, the better the sound insulation. Airborne sound is well absorbed by concrete building parts, while structure-borne sound can be reduced by decoupling or separating building parts (for instance, by a floating screed). > Fig. 5

Fire protection   One of concrete's excellent properties is its resistance to fire. It is essentially regarded as a non-flammable building material (Flammability Class A1). Under heat, concrete retains its strength and does not conduct fire. It does not produce smoke or toxic gases either.

However, under great heat certain stresses arise in concrete that can cause spalling. The reinforcing steel is then exposed, and can begin to melt, which may result in the failure of the entire building part. A similar effect can occur when a fire is being extinguished; the water used to put out the fire makes the building part cool down dramatically, and the stress that ensues can cause concrete to flake off.

Without the need for any additional measures concrete can meet the requirements for fire resistance classes from F30 to F180. Even at high temperatures it is regarded as resistant to smouldering fires and it also provides protection against the heat. Concrete is the most suitable building material for escape stairs (staircases, walls and ceilings). Concrete's resistance to fire can be even further improved through additives. What is called "fire concrete" can withstand temperatures of 500–2000 °C.

Protection against moisture   Concrete is essentially permeable to water vapour. This means that it takes up water or moisture from the surroundings and releases it again after a certain time. It can, however, be made almost water impermeable (waterproof concrete). The relationship to moisture depends upon the concrete mix and proper compacting. A watertight construction made from waterproof concrete is called a "white tank" (> Chapter Building parts, Footings/foundations). Waterproof concrete can also be produced in such a way

Tab. 9: Overview of typical building physics properties

Kind of concrete	Thermal conductivity	Fire resistance class	Flammability class
Aerated concrete	from 0.11 W/(m*K)		
Normal concrete	1.51 to 2.30 W/(m*K)	F30 to F180 without additional measures	A1 – not flammable
Heavy concrete	around 2.30 W/(m*K)		

Airborne sound is contained by the concrete.

Impact sound transmission must be reduced by decoupling at the point of transmission.

Fig. 5: Sound transmission principles

that it is resistant to frost and de-icing agents. There are four exposure categories:

— Moderate water saturation without de-icing agent: XF1
— Moderate water saturation with de-icing agent: XF2
— High water saturation without de-icing agent: XF3
— High water saturation with de-icing agent: XF4

Concrete can also be made in such a way that it can resist chemical attacks for a certain period. To some degree it can be described as acid-resistant. There are three degrees of attack strength:

Resistance to chemicals

— XA1: weak attack
— XA2: moderate attack
— XA3: strong attack

Resistance to chemical attacks is required, for example, when handling process or waste water from industry, in the case of pollution by fumes, or aggressive ground water and soil.

DEFORMATIONS

Deformation can occur in solid or liquid concrete as a result of various physical properties and compositions. Changes in temperature, withdrawal or absorption of water cause the material to change its form considerably. A number of such changes are listed below that can harm concrete and hinder the building part in fulfilling its function.

These processes often cannot be stopped completely, but forward planning can prevent serious losses of function. Alongside the planning, the causes of harmful deformations are generally to be found in the construction or execution, which should always be properly supervised. In particular, care should be taken to ensure that the concrete mix is appropriate and that the concreting process is correctly carried out; the influence of water, air, salts or chemical pollutants must be monitored. The concrete's own movements must be calculated to ensure that the flow of forces can take place unhindered.

Shrinking

Shrinking means the shortening of concrete as it cures and hardens, causing it to lose volume, when hair cracks can develop. The amount by which the volume is reduced is known as shrinkage. Shrinking depends on the moisture levels in the surroundings, the size of the building part, and the concrete mix. With slow curing, shrinkage ranges from 0.2 to 0.5 mm/m.

Early or capillary shrinking

In contrast to normal shrinking this process starts immediately after water is added and is strongly dependent on the water-cement value.

Swelling

Swelling is the opposite of shrinking. It describes the increase in the volume of the concrete as the result of absorbing water.

Attacks

An attack is a chemical reaction and takes place in solid concrete. It results in an increase of volume (example: sulphate attack).

Creep and flow

Creep and flow are deformations that take place under a sustained load. They can be permanent or can diminish over the course of time. They occur primarily with compressive loads, and are caused by the movement of water in the cement stone.

Creep describes a reversible deformation, which diminishes over the course of time and eventually stops. After the structural load is removed the building part returns to its original state (creeping back). Flow is an irreversible deformation that remains even when the load is removed.

The amount of creep is of particular importance for the structural calculations of different building parts. With prestressed concrete, the prestressing means that there is already great compressive load before the element is inserted, the expansion of the stressing steel is reduced and with it the pretension force of the building. In creep, the modulus of elasticity (E) usually plays an important role. It gives the relationship of tension to elastic deformation, which disappears once the load is removed. The modulus of elasticity for normal concrete is between 22,000 and 39,000 E.

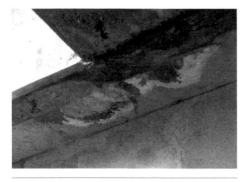

Fig. 6: Efflorescence

DEFECTS

Defects can arise in both fresh and solid concrete during the production and curing process, but can also be due to long-term external influences. Structural loads or temporary loads can also cause defects. These effects generally weaken the entire building part if they exceed the calculated movements in the material. They can arise as the result of mistakes in planning, construction or execution.

One example is lime efflorescence. During the curing process the cement in the concrete separates out hydrated lime. This can dissolve in water and be deposited on the surface. When the water evaporates it remains on the surface and changes into limestone (calcium carbonate). > Fig. 6 The limestone is visible as cloudy patches on the surface of the concrete. Efflorescence occurs above all when water (e.g. rainwater) enters concrete from which the formwork has just been struck or runs between the formwork and the surface of the concrete, when the weather is damp and cold or when other effects cause a temperature difference in the concrete. It can be avoided primarily by introducing measures to protect the fresh concrete. Water should not be allowed to enter the formwork and striking the formwork should only be done in dry weather. Where subsequent treatment of the surface is necessary, foils should be inserted between the concrete and the formwork and damp mats, or appropriate post-treatment agents used.

Efflorescence

Cracks or cracking patterns are included in the calculations of the building parts. > Fig. 7 They result from internal stresses and external forces, i.e. through deformation or the addition of loads. Particular crack patterns are created depending on the consistency or composition of the concrete . It is desirable to create as fine and even a crack pattern as possible, so as to weaken the building part as little as possible. A difference is made between cracks that are close to the surface and separating

Cracks

Fig. 7: Cracks

Fig. 8: Rock pockets

cracks. The latter generally affect the entire cross section or large areas of the building part, whereas surface cracks of 0.1 to 0.4 mm are acceptable. Surface cracks generally only have to be visually removed and have no serious structural implications. Cracks with a structural impact must be avoided from the start by means of adequate reinforcement, incorporation of joints, and the correct concrete mix.

Rock pockets   A rock pocket develops when separation of the aggregate occurs in the fresh concrete. Coarse pieces of aggregate collect at one place. > Fig. 8 They should be avoided by suitable grading of the grain, allowing sufficient mixing time, and by proper compaction.

Concrete bleeding   Bleeding is the term used to describe the appearance of water on the surface of the concrete during the concreting process. By this time the concrete has generally separated. This can be avoided by minimising the w/c value, choosing dense aggregate compositions, and compacting intensively. In addition, the grain size distribution curve should be optimised and a finely ground cement used.

Construction method

As concrete is generally used in the form of reinforced concrete, the concrete building parts are usually loadbearing and form the primary construction, even in large and complex buildings. But concrete can equally be used as a non-loadbearing element that encloses space, and indeed it is even used in furniture for indoors and outdoors. Vertical and horizontal concrete parts can also span large distances. Depending on the shape of the building part, reinforced concrete can be used to take loads that are applied across an area, or point or linear loads. > Fig. 9

There are different ways of producing concrete building parts. Essentially, the elements of the concrete must be mixed together and additives added according to requirements. This mixed, liquid raw state is called "fresh concrete". The proportions of the various contents determine how the concrete is to be worked, the feel of the finished concrete, and whether it suits the requirements at its later location.

Constructional qualities

Production process

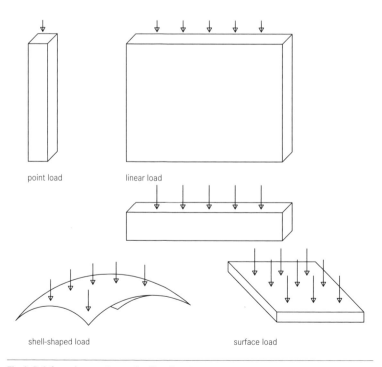

point load   linear load

shell-shaped load   surface load

Fig. 9: Reinforced concrete as a loadbearing structure

Fig. 10: Compacting concrete

Compacting   After mixing, the fresh concrete is poured into a formwork or shuttering in which the reinforcement has already been placed. > Chapter Building material, Reinforcement and Chapter Construction method, Formwork After the concrete has been poured or pumped into the formwork it must be compacted in order to avoid air pockets. There are a number of tried and tested methods of doing this. They include vibrating, tamping and rodding. For these methods an additional compacting appliance is used (e.g. an internal or external vibrator, or a tamper). > Fig. 10 Compacting prevents voids developing between the aggregate and shrinkage cavities between the concrete and the shuttering. Current developments in self-compacting concrete > Chapter Building material, Kinds of concrete mean that tamping may sometimes no longer required. The special properties of this concrete allow an entirely new work process.

The concrete must be introduced in layers and constant care must be taken that it does not separate during concreting or compacting. Tamping should not be carried out for too long but must still fulfil its function. The concreting process should not be interrupted.

During the first few days the freshly introduced concrete must be protected from the weather and environmental influences using films or isolation layers. This not only provides protection against external influences but also contributes to the curing process. The water on the surface must not be allowed to evaporate. Drying out must be prevented by covering, or by introducing water from elsewhere.

○ **Note:** Shrinkage cavities or shrink holes are cavities in the material or indentations in the surface. These can be merely aesthetic imperfections. But from a certain depth and size they are also structurally relevant, as the cover is reduced.

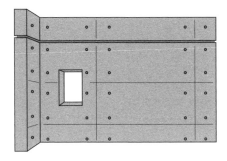
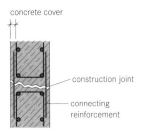

concrete cover

construction joint

connecting reinforcement

Fig. 11: Construction joints

Protection against adverse influences

The surrounding temperature should be between +5 and +30 °C. In the case of heat there is a danger of excessively rapid setting and evaporation. This can be prevented by covering. In the case of frost the cement lime no longer hardens sufficiently and the water in the concrete, which has not yet set, can freeze and cause damage. Here, the use of warm concrete heated in the works or antifreeze agents can help. However, they alter the colour of the concrete, which must be taken into consideration, particularly with exposed concrete.

Wind can also contribute to accelerating the evaporation of the water in fresh concrete. Accordingly, the concrete should not be exposed to excessively strong winds. The same applies to protection against rain to prevent the water content from changing too greatly in the part that is curing.

Within the first 24 hours, concrete sets from a wet to a solid state. It reaches its standard hardness under normal conditions within 28 days and is then described as hardened concrete. During the curing process the concrete is called young or green concrete.

Construction and movement joints

Depending on the size of the building part, the concrete cannot all be poured in a single process but the part must be broken up into different concreting stages. This necessitates construction joints, which should be included in the planning. However, construction joints should be avoided wherever possible as they always represent a weak point. If they are necessary to ensure better bonding they should be produced with a roughened surface (e.g. expanded metal) and protected against damp or the entry of water using sealing tapes or similar.

Movement joints may be needed to avoid tension cracks between two building parts. They must be based on the structural situation and included in the planning and are used above all to deal with expansion or settlement movement. In movement joints the reinforcement is interrupted in order to avoid stress, whereas in construction joints the reinforcement is continued. > Fig. 11

The parameters for the composition of the concrete that were decided upon in the planning must be monitored and checked during the construction work. This can be done by checking the concrete supplier and by taking samples on site.

The bulk density of fresh concrete (kg/dm^3) allows a first assessment of the concrete quality to be made immediately after it has been put in place. It describes the mass of fresh, compacted concrete including pores. It is calculated by weighing a sample piece. Low density means lower strength. The greater the amount of water and pores in the concrete, the lower the bulk density.

The manufacturing process can vary according to the location and the circumstances. Concrete building parts are either produced on site at their final place of use or are precast in a prefabrication works under standardised conditions and later transported to the building site.

IN-SITU CONCRETE

In-situ or cast-in-place concrete means what is called "building site concrete", which is mixed and processed on site. Due to the lack of precision, building site concrete is used only in small amounts and is not the standard case. The term in-situ concrete is now used above all to describe transported concrete that is used most commonly in the building sector. > Fig. 12 This is mixed precisely in the works and then delivered as fresh concrete to the building site where it is poured into the formwork.

The advantages of a building part made of in-situ concrete are the possibilities for strong monolithic connections and the economic use of the material. In-situ concrete is generally used for parts of the building that are not visible or on which there are few demands for the surface appearance. However, this method of construction also has disadvantages. The entire curing process takes place on the building site, i.e. even under unfavourable weather conditions, which can have a major impact on the results of concreting and on the progress on the building site. Extreme temperatures or rainfall often lead to considerable delays and require the construction process to be flexibly planned.

FORMWORK

The formwork or shuttering is the negative form of the concrete building part. The reinforcement steel is placed in it and the liquid concrete then poured into it. It must therefore be dimensioned to withstand the pressure resulting from the introduction of the concrete.

Formwork consists of different parts, generally a formwork system and formwork sheeting. To ensure that the concrete can be released from the formwork after hardening, the sheeting must initially be treated with a release agent (oil, wax, varnish etc.). With standard orthogonal formwork for a wall or a ceiling slab, prefabricated formwork panels are generally used as the formwork sheeting. They are held together by formwork

Fig. 12: Concrete mixer and mixer vehicle

Fig. 13: Exposed concrete with regular anchor holes

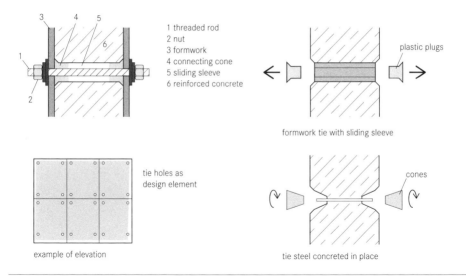

1 threaded rod
2 nut
3 formwork
4 connecting cone
5 sliding sleeve
6 reinforced concrete

plastic plugs

formwork tie with sliding sleeve

tie holes as
design element

example of elevation

cones

tie steel concreted in place

Fig. 14: Formwork anchors

anchors that take the pressure off the concrete. When the formwork is struck (removed from the building part) the holes remain where the anchors were. In building parts that will be visible, the position of these holes should also be considered at the planning stage. > Figs. 13 and 14 They can either be closed or adapted to suit the design concept, but remain visible. The position of openings in and holes through the concrete must also be considered before making the formwork and the necessary adaptations.

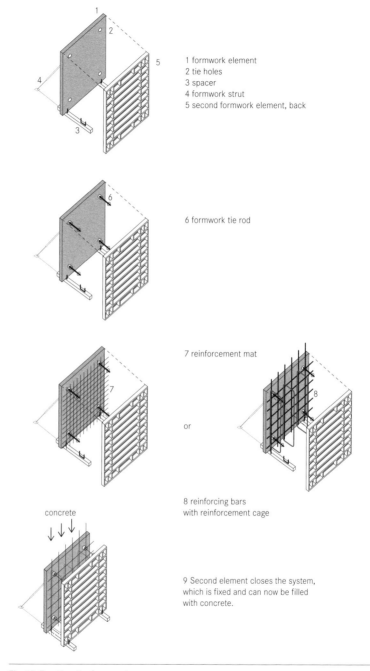

1 formwork element
2 tie holes
3 spacer
4 formwork strut
5 second formwork element, back

6 formwork tie rod

7 reinforcement mat

or

8 reinforcing bars
with reinforcement cage

concrete

9 Second element closes the system,
which is fixed and can now be filled
with concrete.

Fig. 15: Erecting the formwork

Fig. 16: Smooth surface with a large proportion of pores. Rough surface showing marks of board shuttering

The sheeting can be made from a variety of materials that influence the later appearance of the concrete surface. Wood can be used as the formwork sheeting in several different ways. Depending on how it is worked it can produced smooth or rough structures. > Fig. 16 Wood can be used planed, flamed, rough-cut or brushed. The absorbency of the formwork sheeting plays a decisive role. Wood tends to be essentially absorbent: it takes water and air from the concrete while it is curing and thus gives it a particular surface quality. This surface has fewer pores and a more even appearance.

Formwork made of plastic, aluminium or steel is non-absorbent. In contrast to wood, steel or aluminium formwork is expensive but can be used several times. Plastic formwork is inexpensive and durable. Non-absorbent formwork can produce particularly smooth concrete surfaces, but also encourages the formation of pores. As a result, cloudy discolouring or marbled surfaces can develop more quickly. There are also many structured formworks that give designers the freedom to create a structured surface for exposed or fair-faced concrete. > Fig. 17

The different formwork systems are named after the way they are constructed. The most commonly used system is frame formwork. The name is derived from the fact that the formwork panels consist of fixed aluminium or steel frames to which the formwork sheathing (e.g. of wood or plastic) is fixed. These modular elements are suitable for wall and ceiling slab formwork. > Fig. 18 Frame formwork can be erected quickly thanks to its modular system and allows rapid progress to be made with the construction work. Generally speaking, curves or angles are possible only with other systems.

Formwork sheeting

Formwork systems

Fig. 17: Design of different surfaces

A further widely used system is grid formwork, which can also be used for walls and ceiling slabs. It offers a greater degree of flexibility but is somewhat more complex to use, as the formwork system and the sheeting must be mounted as single parts. The girder formwork consists of a grid of girders on which the formwork sheeting is mounted. It can be adjusted precisely and when removed does not leave behind the grid-like pattern of lines caused by frame formwork. This is due to the fact that the sheeting can be inserted in different sizes and materials independently of the formwork construction principle. The beam system is generally built from solid web or lattice girders made of aluminium. > Fig. 19 In connection with the formwork systems, different terms have become part of building site jargon. A girder formwork is also called a "flex formwork", and a premounted ceiling slab formwork is also called a "ceiling table". > Fig. 20

Special building parts require special formwork systems, for instance, column and round formworks. Column formwork is relatively expensive as it must generally be made using a special cross section based on the structural engineer's calculations. The relatively small surface area means that work must be carried out precisely, and a high level of concrete pressure develops within the small formwork. All the columns

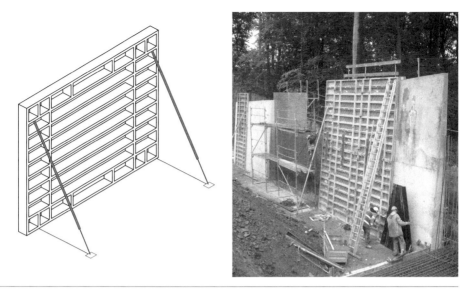

Fig. 18: Frame formwork

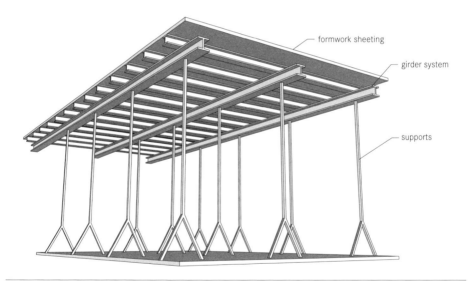

formwork sheeting

girder system

supports

Fig. 19: Girder formwork

within a building should therefore have the same cross section if possible. Even though this may mean that more concrete is used it saves on labour costs and time. The individual formwork can be used several times and the system does not have to be readjusted each time. Round columns are even more difficult as matrices have to be inserted in the sheeting,

Fig. 20: Supporting a ceiling slab formwork

which is generally orthogonal. However, there is an alternative system using cardboard forms. Cardboard tubes that are coated internally allow a round cross section with a smooth surface to be created easily. > Fig. 21 However, large round formwork using the classic system is generally more expensive and must be planned very precisely. Special formwork systems must also be used for building parts such as downstand beams.

Uniform formwork systems generally reach their limitations when complicated, small-scale or individual building parts are involved. Formwork for stairs, for example, is therefore generally produced individually, or entire staircases are concreted in the works. In most cases the standard systems are of limited use only.

○ Climbing or gliding formwork

To produce several floors one after the other, especially in high-rise buildings and tall vertical building parts, a climbing or gliding formwork can prove most efficient.

○ **Note:** A permanent or "lost" formwork is one that cannot be removed after concreting. This can be due to the geometry of the building part or to special circumstances, for instance, when the underside of a floor slab in the ground is no longer accessible.

Fig. 21: Columns in cardboard formwork

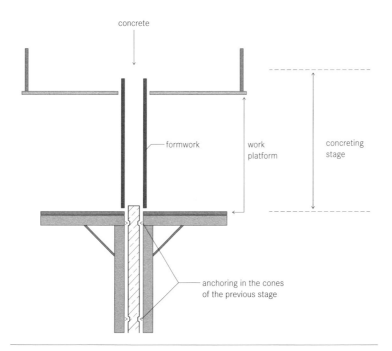

Fig. 22: Climbing formwork

The climbing framework can be used either "crane-assisted" or "self-climbing". Crane-assisted climbing formwork consists of large wall formwork elements that are fixed to console platforms on travelling trolleys. The platforms are anchored in notches in the previously concreted section below and provide a working area for the next section to be concreted. The platform and the formwork are lifted in stages by the crane and thus "climb" upwards. > Fig. 22

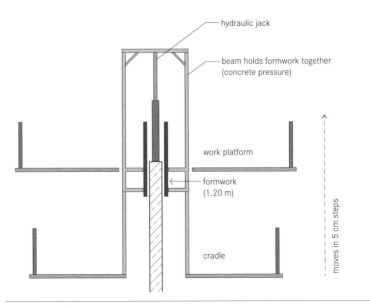

Fig. 23: Gliding formwork

Where it is not possible to use a crane, the formwork moves upwards in stages with the aid of hydraulic lifting mechanisms and is therefore "self-climbing". The concreting stages generally consist of one floor. Both kinds of climbing formwork offer a high level of quality and flexibility during the construction process.

A gliding formwork is used above all for tall building parts with few inserted elements where no great demands are made on the quality of the surface. A continuous wall cross section makes this kind of formwork even more efficient.

The formwork in this case glides in small steps along rods that are centred up the wall and concreting is carried out in layers. > Fig. 23 The work process is continuous and the formwork cannot be changed, cleaned or repaired during it. This kind of formwork ensures that speedy progress of the construction work along with low use of material but on account of its lack of flexibility it demands precise planning from the very start.

CONCRETING PROCESS

Pouring   The actual concreting process is one of the many factors that have a lasting impact, not only on the appearance of the concrete but also on its performance. The standard kind of in-situ concrete is pumped into the formwork on site. Care must be taken in pouring that the drop into the formwork is not too great. In favourable situations concrete can be transported to the place where it is to be used either directly from the

Fig. 24: Pouring concrete

transport vehicle or by means of concrete pumps and crane-assisted concrete buckets. > Fig. 24

Shotcrete is a further method of concreting. A special mix makes it especially flowable and it hardens rapidly, generally due to the addition of an accelerator. Shotcrete allows flat areas of compacted concreted to be made. This method is suitable in particular for improving existing building parts.

A distinction is drawn between the wet and the dry process. In the former, standard mixed concrete with a small aggregate size is used and applied using the appropriate pressure. In the dry spray process the water is first added to the concrete mix in the spray nozzle; this process is particularly suitable for repair work to damaged building parts.

If shotcrete is used to repair damaged building parts it should be noted that the increased amount of concrete increases the weight of the building part. It must be assessed whether the structural capacity remains unimpaired after the improvement work. The use of the shotcrete process frequently makes particular sense for retaining or restoring concrete's fire protection qualities.

In the production, care must be taken to ensure that the old and new concrete areas can bond well. If the concreting stage is interrupted it must be possible to ensure a connection. What is known as "rebound" is the loose material that accumulates on the surface of the shotcrete. It must be carefully brushed off before concreting can recommence.

Shotcrete

Fig. 25: Principles of strengthening a ceiling slab with shotcrete

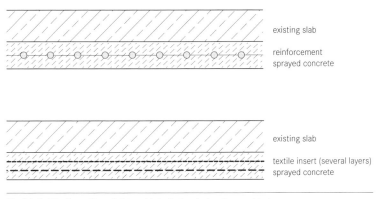

existing slab

reinforcement
sprayed concrete

existing slab

textile insert (several layers)
sprayed concrete

Fig. 26: Soffit of a ceiling slab to which shotcrete has been added

Shotcrete work can be carried out vertically or overhead and consequently it is often used to strengthen areas of ceiling slabs. > Figs. 25 and 26 This work is generally carried out from below. If reinforcement must be used as well, this generally takes the form of lamellae or textile inlays consisting mostly of carbon. Both processes ensure that the carbon structures increase the tensile strength of the building part.

Shotcrete can sometimes be applied to wet surfaces and it is also used in securing building excavation pits.

Tamped concrete   Tamped concrete is named after the concreting process or when tamping is the kind of compaction used. This traditional method is one of the oldest ways of concreting, and is carried out by introducing concrete layer by layer into the formwork and also compacting it layer by layer. The height of the individual layers should not be greater than 15 cm. After the formwork is stripped, the lines of the tamped layers are visible, creating the characteristic visual effect. We can also see certain irregularities, such as denser and less dense areas or collections of aggregate.

Tamped concrete can be used only without reinforcement and therefore the building parts can only handle compression loads or can be used in non-loadbearing situations. Nevertheless, its special aesthetic means tamped concrete is still often used outdoors. Today it is generally not produced in the traditional way but instead a low-mortar concrete is used, which leads to porous areas that create the visual effect required. The aggregate is no longer completely enclosed and is visible externally. This surface can be created by tamping but equally well by compacting in layers.

Spun concrete is produced by compacting the concrete in a hollow mould. The procedure is the same as with pouring concrete, in that the reinforcement is fixed in the formwork and the concrete then added. The rapid rotation of the mould around its own axis presses the concrete against the outer walls. The centrifugal force drives the heavier elements outwards and lets the water flow off inwards. This produces a low water-cement value. Through the compacting process, the concrete acquires a void at the centre of the cross section and an external surface free of bubbles.

Spun concrete

This method of production is particularly suitable for masts, piles, piers or columns. Steel tubes can also be coated with concrete in this way and protected against corrosion. The internal void created is always round, even if the external shape is orthogonal or of a different form. The void is also suitable for taking service runs.

PRECAST ELEMENTS

Precast concrete elements are produced in the factory and delivered to the building site ready to be fitted into position. The advantage of this production method is the precise, clean nature of the process and the quick assembly it allows. Setting times and the weather conditions on the building site need hardly be taken into account at all during the building process. A disadvantage, however, is that the dimensional tolerances are far lower than with in-situ concrete. Precise planning and coordination are required. On the other hand, the precast building method makes it considerably easier to produce fair-faced concrete surfaces. The qualities of the surface can be far more precisely planned and a uniform appearance created, as in the factory the precast concrete parts can be produced under constant conditions without exposure to the weather.

Special properties/ advantages and disadvantages

Fig. 27: Hall-type building made from precast elements

In order to exploit the advantages of both methods, precast and in-site concrete parts are often combined. For example, complex staircase geometries are produced in the factory and combined with an in-situ concrete floor slab, which can incorporate any tolerances that emerge. However, entire building elements can also be produced in the factory. > Fig. 27 In general, though, the size of the elements should take into account the economic aspects of the precast construction method. While building parts of almost any size can be made on site, the question of their transport effectively limits the size of precast elements.

Element construction method
The element construction system is a particularly efficient use of precast elements. Precise production in the works and the repeated use of the same elements can allow work that is very cost and time efficient. The production of the individual elements depends on the size of the modules: for example, on the concreting stages, formwork panel sizes or similar. The joints and anchor holes – which are primarily necessary for transport and which, for visible building parts, must be considered in the planning – are also made in the works. Equally, however, entire prefabricated building cells can be mounted on site.

Filigree elements
Filigree elements are so-called semi-finished parts. This means that filigree prefabricated parts are produced in the factory and then filled on site with fresh concrete. In the case of a wall, for example, the concrete is poured between the two externally visible surfaces. > Figs. 28 and 29

In producing a filigree ceiling slab, the tension reinforcement is fixed in the prefabricated part in the factory. Lattice girders ensure the later bonding with the in-situ concrete. The filigree ceiling slab is placed in position on the building site, providing the lower formwork, and concrete can then be poured on top of it. Bonding means the construction later functions as a bracing panel. A filigree ceiling slab can, however, also be produced as a prestressed building part and can thus allow large spans.

Fig. 28: Filigree elements

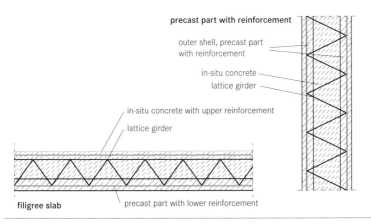

Fig. 29: Filigree floor/ceiling slab

SURFACES

A distinction is drawn between concrete that is used purely for structural reasons and is later covered with other layers such as plaster, and what is called fair-faced or exposed concrete.

Fair-faced concrete

As already mentioned in > Chapter Construction method, Formwork, achieving a smooth exposed concrete surface requires special planning and execution. The composition of the concrete also influences the effect made by the surface. The choice of aggregate tends towards increasingly fine kinds. Different classes are explained in > Chapter Building material, Constituent materials.

■

The quality of fair-faced concrete is also divided into classes; the relevant class should be stated in the specifications. > Tab. 10 The individual criteria for the execution and the surface quality are defined by giving the planned fair-faced concrete class. This is the only way to ensure the quality of the result. The individual criteria also help to achieve the desired overall impression and, where necessary, to introduce changes during the execution phase.

Texture

The texture and formation of the element joints are divided into the criteria T1 to T3. The closed quality of the concrete surface and visibly defective areas along loose joints in the formwork sheeting, which later turn dark, are classified.

Porosity

The porosity of the surface is difficult to check. Classes P1 to P4 limit the maximum amount of porous areas on a test area of the building part. As porosity can differ considerably according to the formwork sheeting used, a distinction is made between absorbent and non-absorbent formwork.

Evenness of shade

Differences in shade are referred to, independently of their cause, by FT1 to FT3. These are only textual formulations that cannot be fixed by precise parameters. Here, too, a distinction is drawn between absorbent and non-absorbent formwork.

Evenness

Evenness classified E1 to E3 relates to general dimensional tolerances in building construction and, where necessary, is adapted to the relevant national standards.

Construction and formwork sheeting joints

The designations AF1 to AF4 primarily limit the surface offsets between two formwork elements that are acceptable.

Test surface and formwork sheeting class

The formwork sheeting is divided into the classes SHK1 to SHK3. They describe the condition of the sheeting and are relatively clearly distinct from each other. The relevant construction firm is responsible for maintaining the sheeting class. To enable architects to define their concept for the finished surface as precisely as possible, the sheeting class can be determined individually and further criteria added.

Additives

The nature of the surface and the visual appearance of the building part can be manipulated by the use of additives. In general these do not have any major effects on the basic properties of the concrete but have a considerable impact on the design. For instance, pigments can be used

■ **Tip:** For a smooth surface quality the w/c value should not be greater than 0.5, the cement content should be above 350 kg/m^3, and the proportion of aggregate grain to cement should not be greater than 6:1.

Tab. 10: Fair-faced concrete classes and their relationship to demands

Fair-faced concrete class	Demand profile	Building parts (examples)	Texture	Porosity		Evenness of shade		Evenness	Construction and formwork	Test area	Formwork sheeting class	Costs
				Absorbent	Non-absorbent	Absorbent	Non-absorbent					
SB 1	Low demands	Basement walls, walls of rooms with commercial use	T1	P1		FT1	FT1	E1	AF1	Optional	SHK1	Low
SB 2	Normal demands	Staircase walls, retaining walls	T2	P2	P1	FT2	FT2	E1	AF2	Recommended	SHK2	Medium
SB 3	High design demands	Facades in building construction (most commonly used class)	T2	P3	P2	FT2	FT2	E2	AF3	Strongly recommended	SHK2	High
SB 4	Especially high design demands	Representative building parts in building construction, for representative prominent buildings (built on the basis of SB 3 with somewhat more stringent requirements)	T3	P4	P3	FT3	FT2	E3	AF4	Required	SHK3	Very high

to give concrete a colour. The colour created is homogeneous and in principle there are no boundaries to the shade that can used. By means of coloured aggregates or granulates, small-scale accents can be introduced which, depending on the grain size, influence the appearance of the surface as a whole.

In addition to design with colour, translucency can be produced or highlights introduced using other materials. For example, optical glass fibres worked into concrete can conduct light through the solid building material. The concrete becomes translucent. Depending on the arrangement and density of the fibres, different appearances and intensities can be produced. Translucent concrete can be used both indoors and outdoors. > Fig. 30

Fig. 30: Translucent concrete

Fig. 31: Examples of surface patterns and structures

The addition of marble or glass, for example, can also place special features. Shimmering effects or special kinds of surfaces can be achieved, depending on the grain size of the additive and the mix proportions.

Formwork The formwork sheeting plays an important role in the design of the concrete surface. Depending on the material chosen it can, through its absorbent or non-absorbent quality, produce a smooth or a structured surface. Non-absorbent sheeting generally produces a smooth surface, which, however, tends towards a certain degree of porosity. Clients and architects often require the concrete to have a particularly even appearance.

Absorbent formwork sheeting ensures that the structure of the material used for the sheeting is transferred to the surface of the concrete. For example, the grain of wooden formwork can be shown on the concrete or other materials imitated.

A further way of creating a surface structure is to insert matrices into the formwork. Generally made of plastic, these elements can produce almost any kind of motif or pattern. There are almost no restrictions to a designer's imagination. Other objects from the everyday world or nature can also be inserted into the formwork for design purposes. > Fig. 31

Later surface Even after production the appearance of the surface of a concrete
treatment building part can be manipulated. Such treatment methods can be roughly subdivided into chemical, manual, technical and mechanical processes. > Tab. 11

Chemical treatment methods include acid washing or the commonly used exposed aggregate process. In acid washing a diluted acid is used to remove the outer cement skin. Exposed aggregate concrete, in contrast, is ground with retarders allowing the different aggregates to appear. > Fig. 32 Photo concrete can depict precise graphic designs. Using a

Fig. 32: Exposed aggregate concrete facade

Tab. 11: Surface treatment methods

Chemical treatment	Acid washing with diluted acid	Exposed aggregate concrete	Photo concrete	
Manual treatment	Bush hammering: using bush hammer or chisel	Chiselling: using point chisel and hammer	Droving: using drove chisel or machine	Bush hammering: using compressed air chisel
Technical treatment	Sand or flame blasting			
Mechanical treatment	Polishing	Grinding		

silk-screen process, light and dark colour gradients can be produced on the surface.

Skilled manual treatment processes are based on the principle of removing the outermost concrete layer with the help of various tools. Bush hammers or chisels, pointed chisels and hammers can be used. They produce a rough surface that is lighter in colour. In bush-hammering surfaces and edges can be worked up to a depth of 6 mm, whereas with pointed chisels a depth of 10 mm can be achieved. Droving is carried out with a machine or a drove chisel and creates a regularly structured surface. In bush-hammering a compressed air chisel can be used, which creates a somewhat coarser surface. > Fig. 33

Technical treatments include the use of sand or flame blasting which again changes the outermost layer of the concrete. In contrast, mechanical treatment is carried out by polishing or grinding the concrete and subsequently varnishing or waxing it. This creates a smooth, fine surface.

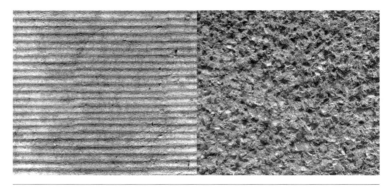

Fig. 33: Droved (left) and bush-hammered (right) surface

When planning a building part that is to be constructed thought should also be given to its ageing process. Soiling through environmental effects, fumes, rainwater or similar can cause massive changes to the appearance after just a short time. In planning, the orientation and wind directions should be taken into account as well as the flow pattern of rainwater in order to avoid smears. The same applies to the inclination of the building part and the nature of its surfaces. In addition to their design effects these can also be manipulated in terms of their capacities.

For instance, a watertight surface can be created by using silicone resins that impregnate the pores close to the surface. This process is called hydrophobing. The building part still remains permeable but the water simply runs off.

There are certain treatments that can be used to provide protection against graffiti, which cannot generally be covered over by a simple coat of paint. What is called a "sacrificial coating" involves the treatment of the concrete surface with waxes. It is easy to clean but this layer is "sacrificed" to the cleaning process. After cleaning has been carried out the wax layer must be reapplied to the entire surface. An alternative is a permanent coating. It lasts for longer than a sacrificial coating but reduces the diffusivity of the wall.

Building parts

As with other building materials, many requirements for concrete are regulated by standards and guidelines. The building parts must be planned, checked and approved, before they are finally constructed. The individual building parts are considered below and their nature explained.

Placing building parts together always involves connecting different layers such as seals or protective films and ensuring that they function perfectly. With regard to concrete, there are a number of special aspects. The constructional connection of two building parts made of reinforced concrete is generally done by means of connecting or projecting reinforcement. This varies according to the production method. Precast elements and in-situ concrete can be easily connected with each other, as can two in-situ concrete parts. To connect two precast elements, special bearing parts must be formed.

FOOTINGS / FOUNDATIONS

The function of the foundation is to transfer the load of a building to the ground. Here it is necessary to investigate the bearing capacity of the soil or the loadbearing layer. Together with the structural system of the building, a suitable foundation for transferring the building loads to the ground is then planned.

Every foundation must be made frost free. In central Europe a depth of 80 cm from the surface of the ground must be guaranteed. If a foundation does not itself reach this depth, either a frost skirt must be added or the foundation must be made deeper. > Fig. 34

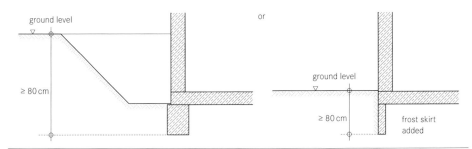

Fig. 34: Frost-free foundation

Tab. 12: Possible kinds of water in the ground

Non-pressing water		
Soil moisture	Moisture that is bound into the soil. Arises, e.g. by infiltration of rainfall into water permeable ground.	
Seepage water	Water that gravity causes to move in the direction of the groundwater.	
	Non-accumulating seepage water	Flows off almost unobstructed (gravel or sandy soils).
	Standing seepage water	Water accumulates at times above less permeable layers of ground.
Pressing water		
Back water	Water that accumulates in less permeable ground layers and, unlike seepage water, does not soon flow off, but exerts pressure on the building part.	
Layer water	If in soil with generally poor permeability there are layers with better water permeability, the water flows in such a layer towards the building and exerts pressure on it.	
Ground water	Water table in the ground, exerts pressure on the building where it extends down into the ground water area.	

Tab. 13: The demands made on a white tank

Demand class 1	Pressing and non-pressing water and at times standing seepage water
Demand class 2	Wet ground and non-accumulating seepage water
Use class A	No ingress of water
Use class B	Damp areas at joints or cracks are accepted

Sealing/ waterproofing

The parts of the building in contact with the ground must be protected against moisture. In general a distinction is made between non-pressing and pressing water. > Tab. 12

In the case of non-pressing water a normal seal against ground moisture, for example, a bitumen coating, can be used. Where there is pressing water the foundation must be protected against the entry of water. This can be done by means of a bituminous sealant (black tank) or watertight reinforced concrete parts (white tank).

A black tank is produced by constructing the building parts in contact with the ground in several layers. In addition, (black) sealing membranes must be applied – giving the black tank its name. > Fig. 35

A white tank is made from waterproof concrete and essentially needs no further sealing layer. Diffusion or capillary effects can, however, influence the watertightness of the white tank. It is not absolutely watertight and, depending on the demands made on it, must be augmented by special additives and very precisely made joints. There are different ways of making watertight joints. Thermoplastic or elastomeric joint tapes can be used or metal waterstops can be inserted; on the other hand, joints are often sealed after they have been made.

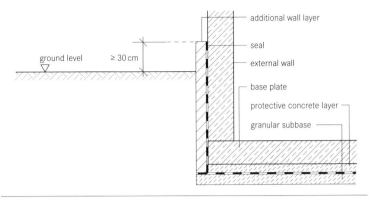

ground level   ≥ 30 cm

additional wall layer

seal

external wall

base plate

protective concrete layer

granular subbase

Fig. 35: Building a black tank

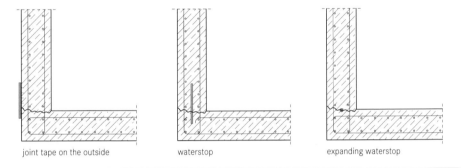

joint tape on the outside   waterstop   expanding waterstop

Fig. 36: Sealing joints

Joint tapes protect against the entry of water into building joints without continuous reinforcement, whereas waterstops (coated or uncoated) are generally used for building parts with continuous reinforcement, where they are concreted into the adjoining building parts. > Fig. 36

A white tank must meet particular requirements. The base slab and the sides must be at least 25 cm thick and, depending on the function and the soil condition, the criteria for particular demand and use classes must be met. > Tab. 13

○

○ **Note:** Joint tapes or metal waterstops bridge the joints between different concreted sections, which would otherwise allow the entry of water despite homogeneous watertight concrete. These generally include the transition from the foundation slab to the basement walls but also the different concreting stages in the walls themselves or even sump pits or other penetrations.

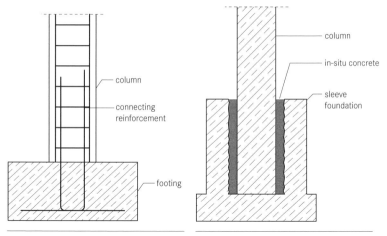

Fig. 37: Connecting reinforcement for a column

column
connecting reinforcement
footing

Fig. 38: Sleeve foundation

column
in-situ concrete
sleeve foundation

Alternatives that require product-related approval include injection hoses and expanding waterstops. These waterstops can be inserted, for example, between the reinforcement rods. They swell when they come into contact with water and seal the joint. In all cases the arrangement of the reinforcement must be suited to the joint sealing method used.

■ Pad foundation   Pad foundations transfer point loads from the building such as the loads of a column. They can be cast on site or made as prefabricated elements. For rigidly fixed columns the connection is made by means of connecting reinforcement. > Fig. 37

A variation of the point foundation is the sleeve foundation > Figs. 38 and 39, which is also used for precast columns. The column is concreted into the sleeve, forming a rigid connection.

Strip foundations   The function of a strip foundation is similar to that of a pad foundation: transferring linear loads from the building. Strip foundations are therefore generally made under loadbearing walls. > Fig. 40 According to the dimensions and the load, strip foundations can be made with or without reinforcement. In very simple load situations, foundations without

> ■ **Tip:** If rooms located in the ground are intended for a high-quality use so that the entrance of damp must be prevented at all costs, the combination of two processes (e.g. white tank with black external sealing layer or joint sheets and waterstops) can make sense. Sealing poorly constructed tanks after they have been built is difficult.

Fig. 39: Sleeve foundations

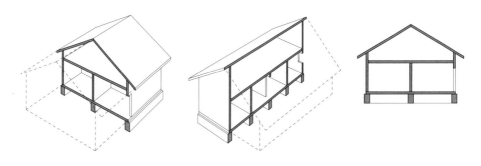

Fig. 40: Laying out strip foundations

reinforcement can be made using suitably dimensioned excavations that are simply filled with concrete, without the need for formwork. When foundations have to be reinforced and made in formwork, this should be taken into account in calculating the total amount of excavation work, which should also include a sufficient surrounding area for working.

Generally speaking, a raft footing can be made as a slab foundation. A suitably dimensioned ground slab transfers the loads to the ground. It can be used where the soil bearing capacity is poor, as well as on ground where the bearing capacity is good. The even distribution of the load can prevent settlement and cracks. The raft foundation must be laid on a granular subbase and an anti-capillary layer. The granular subbase provides a smooth surface on which to pour the concrete and functions as the lower formwork. It offers the only possibility of ensuring that the lower reinforcement has sufficient concrete cover. > Fig. 41

Raft footing

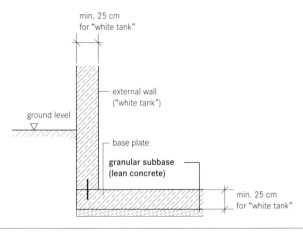

min. 25 cm
for "white tank"

external wall
("white tank")

ground level

base plate

**granular subbase
(lean concrete)**

min. 25 cm
for "white tank"

Fig. 41: Raft foundation with granular subbase

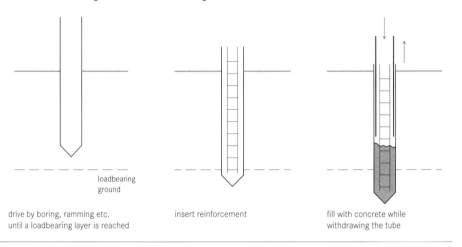

loadbearing
ground

drive by boring, ramming etc.
until a loadbearing layer is reached

insert reinforcement

fill with concrete while
withdrawing the tube

Fig. 42: Making a piled footing

Pile footing

In soils with poorer bearing capacity or where the bearing layer lies deeper, pile footings are used. > Fig. 42 The piles can be precast, or made in situ or as composite piles. With the in-situ method the concrete is poured directly into the bored hole. Prefabricated piles are made in the factory as a whole or as individual parts. In the composite system a bearing member of steel or concrete is inserted into the bored hole and grouted with cement mortar. The bearing members are inserted by means of ramming, boring, flushing, pressing, vibrating or by using screws. The depth of the piles can also be combined with the use of geothermal energy. Depending on the nature of the ground and of the building there are various special forms of piled footings and they can be combined individually with other kinds of footings.

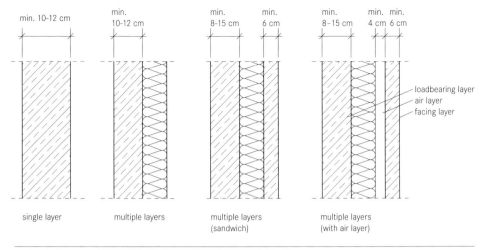

| min. 10-12 cm | min. 10-12 cm | min. 8-15 cm | min. 6 cm | min. 8-15 cm | min. 4 cm | min. 6 cm |

loadbearing layer
air layer
facing layer

| single layer | multiple layers | multiple layers (sandwich) | multiple layers (with air layer) |

Fig. 43: Principles of wall construction

WALL

In accordance with its shape, a wall takes up linear loads and can be made in different ways. In additional to vertical loads the plate effect of a wall enables it to provide bracing and to take horizontal loads. Concrete walls can also be made as space enclosing, non-loadbearing elements, or as front-hung facade elements.

Where they form the external skin, reinforced concrete walls require insulation in order to meet thermal insulation standards. The minimum thickness of a reinforced concrete wall made of in-situ concrete is 10 cm, as long as it is under a continuous ceiling slab. Otherwise it must be at least 12 cm thick. For reasons of sound insulation, concrete walls in housing are generally 18 cm thick.

Prefabricated wall elements can consist of one or more layers. A common element is the sandwich element, which, when delivered from the factory, meets all the structural, building physics and design demands. It consists of a loadbearing layer, insulation and a facing layer; an air layer can be added if required. Openings and conduits for services can also be made in the factory. > Fig. 43

Prefabricated wall elements

Reinforced concrete walls produced as precast elements must, if under a continuous ceiling slab, have a minimum thickness of 8 cm, and if outside at least 10 cm.

If the precast element consists of a bearing layer, insulation and facing layer, the bearing layer must be between 8 cm and 15 cm thick, depending on the load. It is dimensioned according to structural requirements, and reinforced. The facing layer is generally around 6 cm thick. If the surface is to be treated later > Chapter Construction method, Surfaces, the outer layer must be made somewhat thicker so that, despite the surface removed, the necessary concrete cover is still provided.

The maximum dimensions of precast elements depend on the means of production, transport and fitting. The usual dimensions are between 4 and 10 m. In fluctuating temperatures, the facing layer should not be exposed to any stress. A panel should therefore not be any larger than 15 m², with a maximum width of 5 m. Under some circumstances there can be more joints in the facing layer than in the bearing layer.

COLUMN

Reinforced columns can transfer enormous point loads. However, they are less suitable for taking horizontal forces and should be designed primarily to take compressive stress. The production and concreting of a column requires a certain planning basis and guidelines that are explained in the > Chapter Construction method, Formwork and Concreting process. Depending on the formwork chosen, the design and economic constraints, there are a number of different cross sections that can be selected for columns. > Fig. 44

Prefabricated columns
Columns can also be made as precast elements. Where there is a connection to a beam or ceiling element that is also precast, the transition from column to beam or ceiling slab cannot be monolithic and bearing areas must be formed instead. > Fig. 45

A further variation is the composite column, which in principle consists of a steel beam section that is filled with concrete. In this version

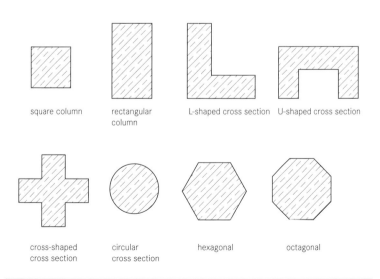

square column   rectangular column   L-shaped cross section   U-shaped cross section

cross-shaped cross section   circular cross section   hexagonal   octagonal

Fig. 44: Typical column cross sections

Fig. 45: Prefabricated columns

no formwork is necessary and columns with very slender cross sections can be made. Conversely, a steel beam can also be encased in concrete to create a loadbearing core. The minimum dimension for in-situ columns is 20 cm, and 15 cm for prefabricated columns, independent of the type of cross section chosen.

BEAM

Beams can be made in very different dimensions. They can be used to span smaller openings (lintels) or as part of a frame construction. Equally, a beam can serve as the bearing or substructure for a ceiling, and can be made as an upstand or downstand beam. Where the beams and ceiling slab are made monolithic we speak of a T-beam or slab-and-beam system. > Chapter Building parts, Ceiling/floor slab This system is made of in-situ concrete and generally in a single work process. The effective structural height of the T-beams is that of the actual beam plus the thickness of the slab. > Fig. 46

The beams generally have solid cross sections. To simplify production and the formwork, rectangular cross sections are generally used. In the prefabricated system profiles such T- and I-beams can be used to reduce weight. Here, thought should be given to which method of production and type of cross section is the most economic and efficient. > Fig. 47

Recent developments in high-performance concrete allow thinner and thinner sections, and make hollow sections possible as well; this enables both concrete and weight to be saved.

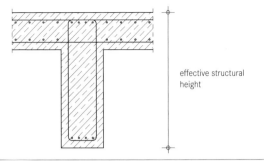

effective structural height

Fig. 46: Structural system of the T-beam

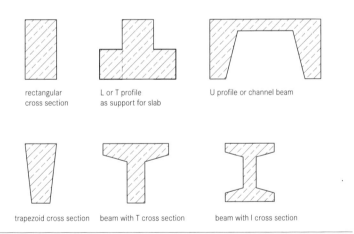

rectangular cross section

L or T profile as support for slab

U profile or channel beam

trapezoid cross section

beam with T cross section

beam with I cross section

Fig. 47: Typical beam cross sections

Beams that are adapted to the form of the moment curve can also be made, which both match the ideal flow of forces and allow other roof forms with slopes. > Fig. 48

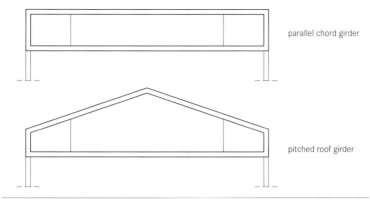

parallel chord girder

pitched roof girder

Fig. 48: Beam forms

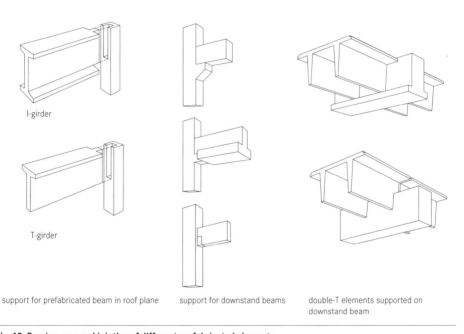

I-girder

T-girder

support for prefabricated beam in roof plane   support for downstand beams   double-T elements supported on downstand beam

Fig. 49: Bearing area and jointing of different prefabricated elements

To connect different prefabricated elements, bearing areas have to be made. > Fig. 49

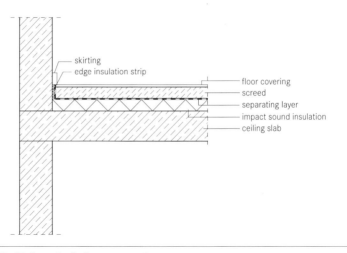

Fig. 50: Example of a floor construction

skirting
edge insulation strip
floor covering
screed
separating layer
impact sound insulation
ceiling slab

CEILING / FLOOR SLAB

In concrete construction a ceiling slab can be made using different systems. The standard method is the in-situ ceiling slab. The formwork is made using a ceiling "table", the reinforcement put in place, and the concrete then poured over it. However, precast or filigree elements can equally well be used. > Chapter Construction method, Precast elements Various layers can be used for acoustic decoupling and to make the finished floor. > Fig. 50 A ceiling slab is a horizontal plate and therefore as well as transferring forces in a vertical direction it also always has a bracing effect in the horizontal plane. It can be made with or without prestressing. Ceiling slabs in normal multi-storey building (housing) are generally made with a thickness of 18 cm and more. Bearing points and the formation of monolithic connections differ according to the nature of the wall material. > Figs. 51 and 52

Reinforced concrete can be used most efficiently in creating different structural systems. Every form of beam, beamed ceiling slab, coffered ceiling slab or T-beam and slab can be made. By using slender downstand beams at close centres > Chapter Building parts, Beam, monolithic ribbed slabs can be made. > Fig. 53 The ribs, which are spaced 30–70 cm apart, run in the main loadbearing direction and are more slender than standard downstand beams. In precast construction, what are known as double T-beams are often used. These consist of two ribs and the projecting ceiling slab. The joints are either filled with in-situ concrete on the building site or a top concrete layer is poured over them. > Fig. 54

If the ribs run in both directions they form a coffered ceiling. > Fig. 55 The coffered ceiling slab can span in two directions. Here, too, the monolithic connection with the ceiling ensures that the system has a highly

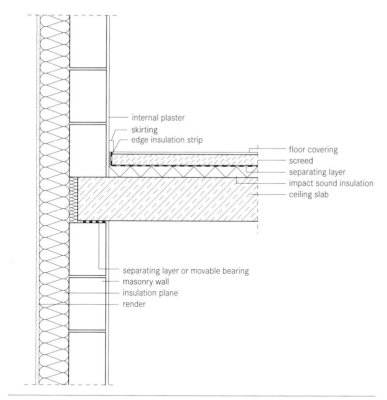

- internal plaster
- skirting
- edge insulation strip
- floor covering
- screed
- separating layer
- impact sound insulation
- ceiling slab

- separating layer or movable bearing
- masonry wall
- insulation plane
- render

Fig. 51: Ceiling slab resting on masonry wall

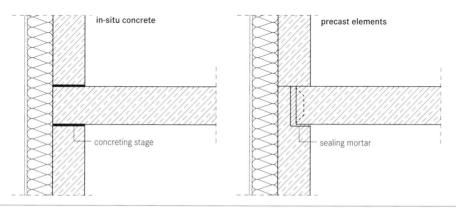

in-situ concrete

concreting stage

precast elements

sealing mortar

Fig. 52: Ceiling slab resting on reinforced concrete wall

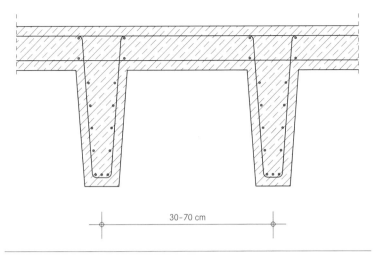

Fig. 53: Ribbed slab

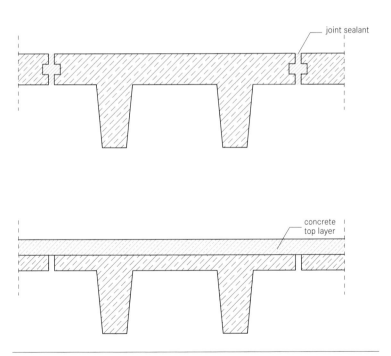

Fig. 54: Double T-beam slab

Fig. 55: Coffered ceiling slab   Fig. 56: Beam grillage

efficient loadbearing capacity. However, production is elaborate, particularly making the formwork. The ribs can theoretically be adapted to the flow of forces in the building part, but this may further complicate production.

Where the ribs are made without a ceiling slab, for instance, in order to make transparent floors and roofs, the system resembles that of a beam grillage. > Fig. 56 As in steel construction, this enables the loadbearing effect of a flat surface to be achieved using linear building elements.

Flat ceiling slabs that rest only on columns and require no downstand beams are also possible. They must be made somewhat thicker and, generally, are used for spans between 7 and 8 m, as for larger spans their massiveness makes them no longer economically viable. Flat ceiling slabs are particularly useful for free floor plans, as they create soffits without any interruptions and are therefore very flexible.

To handle the enormous forces that develop at the columns when a flat slab is used, punching shear reinforcement is often required. A higher amount of reinforcement is laid around the column, which means that columns for flat ceilings cannot generally be positioned directly at the edge of the slab or at the facade. > Fig. 57 One version that offers a way of dealing with bearing loads is the mushroom slab. > Fig. 58 The slab rests on columns that have a specially shaped ("mushroom") column head that distributes the loads better. It allows structurally optimised use of the slab but the formwork for the columns is considerably more elaborate.

In order to reduce mass and weight, hollow elements can be laid in the cross-sectional area that is not structurally required (hollow core floor), depending on the particular structural demands.

Hollow core ceiling/floor slabs can be prestressed or made with slack reinforcement. They have continuous voids in the longitudinal direction and can therefore be spanned uniaxially. The slabs are firmly fixed to each other by interlocking, cross and longitudinal reinforcement, and by filling the joints. In addition to using joint filler there are also kinds

Hollow core planks

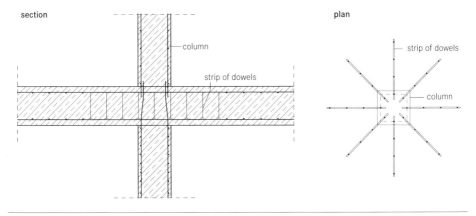

section   plan

Fig. 57: Punching shear reinforcement

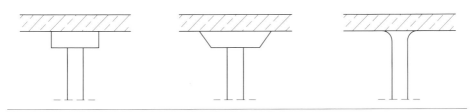

Fig. 58: Mushroom head columns

in which a top layer of concrete is added that either has a load distributing function or also helps to carry the load. Depending on how it is made the slab can function as a plate and can also take horizontal forces.

Prestressed hollow core floors allow wide spans with a low slab thickness. They are reinforced in the longitudinal direction with steel strands alone; the necessary tension reinforcement is positioned near the underside of the slab in the continuous solid webs. The elements are usually 80–120 cm wide and 16–40 cm thick.

Thanks to the prefabrication of the elements and the ease of moving them by means of a mobile or building crane directly from the transport vehicle, hollow core slabs ensure a speedy and economic construction process. They can be placed in position without propping. They can be connected with steel, reinforced concrete or masonry walls. The continuous ring beam, made of concrete, is most important. > Figs. 59, 60 and 61

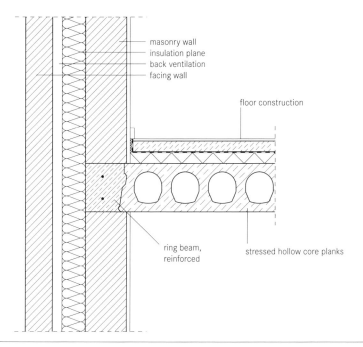

- masonry wall
- insulation plane
- back ventilation
- facing wall

floor construction

ring beam, reinforced

stressed hollow core planks

Fig. 59: Connections of hollow core planks to masonry wall

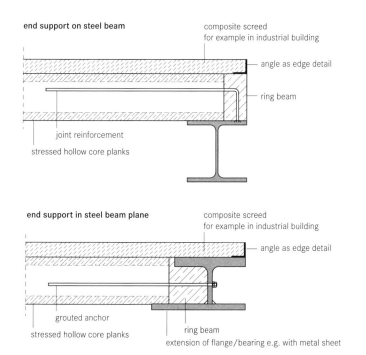

end support on steel beam

composite screed
for example in industrial building

angle as edge detail

ring beam

joint reinforcement

stressed hollow core planks

end support in steel beam plane

composite screed
for example in industrial building

angle as edge detail

grouted anchor

stressed hollow core planks

ring beam

extension of flange / bearing e.g. with metal sheet

Fig. 60: Connections of hollow core planks to steel construction

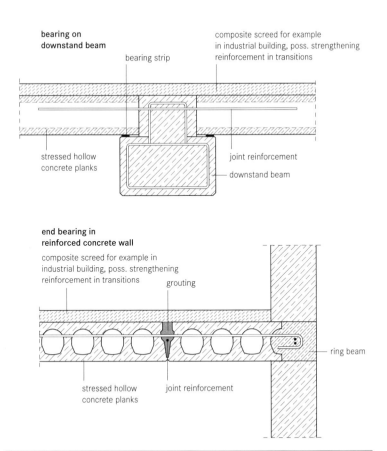

bearing on downstand beam

bearing strip

composite screed for example in industrial building, poss. strengthening reinforcement in transitions

stressed hollow concrete planks

joint reinforcement

downstand beam

end bearing in reinforced concrete wall

composite screed for example in industrial building, poss. strengthening reinforcement in transitions

grouting

stressed hollow concrete planks

joint reinforcement

ring beam

Fig. 61: Connections of hollow core planks to reinforced concrete wall and downstand beam

The use of reinforced concrete allows optimal exploitation of material and loadbearing capacity and also the integration of other building functions. For instance, cross-sectional areas with no structural function can be combined with concrete core activation or other kinds of services.

○ **Note:** Concrete core activation or building part activation is a system in which heating or cooling pipes filled with water or air run through the concrete building parts. The system uses concrete's high density and storage capacity to regulate the temperature in the building. Through the pipes laid in the concrete heat or cold is given off later.

Planning the openings is of equal importance in the design of both walls and ceiling slabs. They must be considered in drawing the formwork and reinforcement plans and in the production. In positioning ceiling openings in particular, the structural system must be carefully considered, as openings should not be in areas where the slab is subject to the greatest stress. In optimised systems such as prestressed concrete hollow core planks, the possibility of making additional openings later is very restricted. During the planning stage careful thought must be given to the direction in which the ceiling slab spans, how the downstand beam and reinforcement systems run and where, if necessary, further strengthening has to be calculated.

ROOF AND ROOF PARAPET

In the form of a flat roof, a reinforced concrete slab can form the final terminating part of a building and carry the necessary insulation and sealing layers. In construction terms, concrete pitched roofs can also be made, so that the standard change to timber construction for the roof structure is often unnecessary.

With a flat roof in particular, proper sealing and a continuous insulation layer must be ensured in order to avoid causing any damage in building physics terms. Like other roofs, a reinforced concrete roof is made from a loadbearing layer, a moisture barrier, the insulation, and the final sealing with a protective layer. A flat roof can use the loadbearing systems of the ceiling slabs. Particular attention must be given to drainage. Proper falls of at least 2% must be ensured. The roof water drainage can also run through the inside of the building. In this case it penetrates the sealing layer in some places, which must be detailed and made with great care. > Fig. 64 The fall is not generally made with the loadbearing element but is produced later by an additional concrete layer laid to falls or by sloping insulation. The roof parapet can be made in a number of different ways. It can, for instance, be a monolithic upstand but it can also be separated thermally. This alters the construction thicknesses through additional insulation measures. > Figs. 62 and 63

THERMAL SEPARATION

One common joint is the connection of a projecting element, such as a balcony slab. Here, the thermal separation of the element presents a particular challenge as it penetrates the outer skin. A number of manufacturers have examined this problem and have developed elements that can both insulate and provide the structural connection.

As with roof parapet walls there are essentially two ways in which this connection can be made. Either what is known as an Isokorb is made to ensure thermal separation > Fig. 65, or the balcony slab must be insulated on both sides. > Fig. 66 Naturally, this latter solution requires additional material and also has a visual effect on the final thickness of the slab.

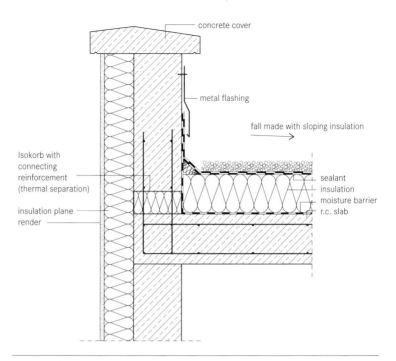

concrete cover

metal flashing

fall made with sloping insulation →

Isokorb with
connecting
reinforcement
(thermal separation)

insulation plane
render

sealant
insulation
moisture barrier
r.c. slab

Fig. 62: Roof parapet wall, thermally separated

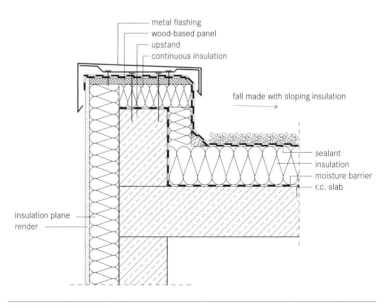

metal flashing
wood-based panel
upstand
continuous insulation

fall made with sloping insulation →

sealant
insulation
moisture barrier
r.c. slab

insulation plane
render

Fig. 64: Internal drainage

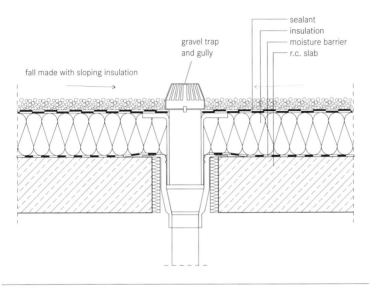

fall made with sloping insulation

gravel trap
and gully

sealant
insulation
moisture barrier
r.c. slab

Fig. 63: Roof parapet as upstand wall

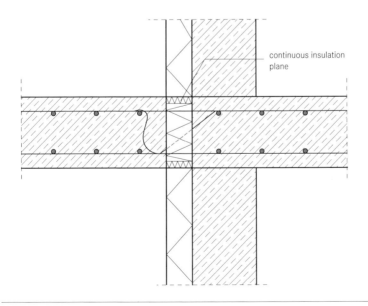

continuous insulation
plane

Fig. 65: Thermally separated cantilever

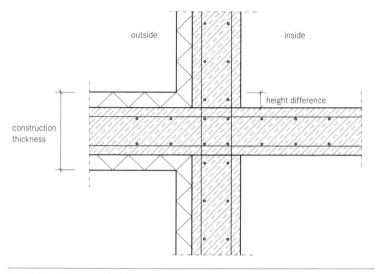

outside   inside

height difference

construction
thickness

Fig. 66: Insulation on both sides

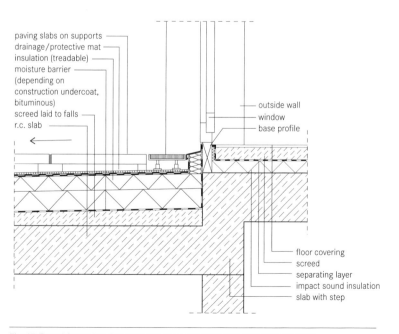

paving slabs on supports
drainage / protective mat
insulation (treadable)
moisture barrier
(depending on
construction undercoat,
bituminous)
screed laid to falls
r.c. slab

outside wall
window
base profile

floor covering
screed
separating layer
impact sound insulation
slab with step

Fig. 67: Transition to loggia with reinforced concrete slab folded downwards

If the slab is not a cantilever but, for example, a loggia above a living room, there are great differences in the construction layers between inside and outside. Here, the designer must react at an early stage. > Fig. 67 If, for design reasons, it is not possible to fold the reinforced concrete slab downwards, then steps or suspended ceilings must be used.

STAIRCASES

Its particular geometry and function makes the staircase a most complex building element. Heights, regulations about the dimensions of the steps, and the choice of material play important roles. Precise execution of the soffits and surfaces is also important. Concrete offers good opportunities in terms of design, loadbearing capacity and production. It meets all the requirements for an escape staircase with regard to fire and heat resistance, acoustic decoupling, and geometry.

Staircases made of in-situ concrete can be adapted on site to any floor plan. The different tolerances of building parts already produced can be handled easily. In contrast, precast staircases allow no departures from the design dimensions, but they can be produced quickly and cleanly. It should be ensured that the stairwell is sufficiently large to allow a precast flight of steps to be hoisted into the building. Naturally, the main focus of attention is on the basic regulations about the dimensions of treads and risers, numbers of steps without an intermediate landing etc. > Tab. 14

Tab. 14: Basic dimensions for staircases

Building kind	Kind of stairs	Minimum usable width [cm]	Rise r min. [mm]	Tread t max. [mm]	Tread t min. [mm]
Residential building with up to two dwellings	Stairs required by the building regulations	80	140	200	230
	Stairs not required by the building regulations (additional stairs)	50	140	210	210
Buildings in general	Stairs required by the building regulations	100	140	190	260
	Stairs not required by the building regulations (additional stairs)	50	140	210	210

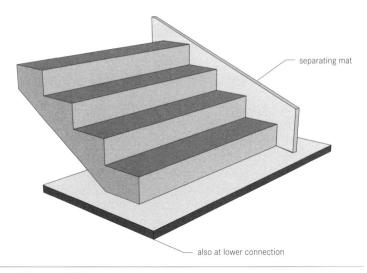

separating mat

also at lower connection

Fig. 68: Decoupled flight of steps

Particular attention should be paid to the acoustic decoupling of flights of steps and landings. Just as with the thermal separation of projecting building elements, an Isokorb can be used, or a simple footfall sound decoupling.

There are several possibilities and combinations as regards acoustic decoupling. Both the flights of steps and the landings must be decoupled. The flights of steps can be separated from the staircase side wall by a simple joint that interrupts the transmission of sound without need for any further measures. This joint should not be wider than 6 cm. If the flights of steps are to adjoin the side walls directly, sound decoupling mats can be inserted between the flights and the wall. > Fig. 68

Apart from decoupling from the wall, the upper and lower connection of the flight of steps must also be decoupled. At the foot of the stairs a mat can also be used. The upper connection to the landing can be made by means of a shaped bearing or an Isokorb.

Precast staircases can be connected to a bearing point that has already been made on the landing. > Fig. 69 For in-situ concrete, suitable products with integrated connecting reinforcement can be used. > Fig. 70

The staircase landing can also be decoupled in a number of different ways. Essentially, decoupling by means of a standard floor construction with a floating screed is possible and sensible, as it allows the

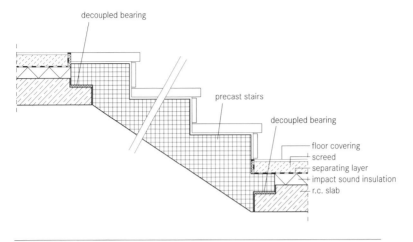

Fig. 69: Precast staircase at landings with floating screed

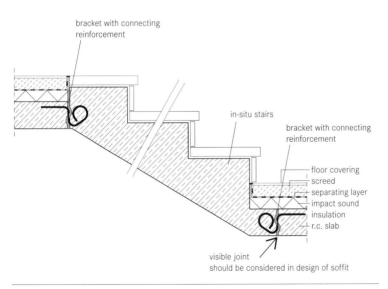

Fig. 70: Upper and lower connection of an in-situ flight of steps

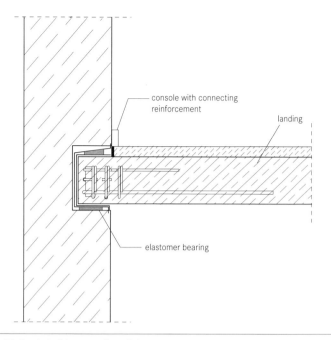

Fig. 71: Bracket with connecting reinforcement

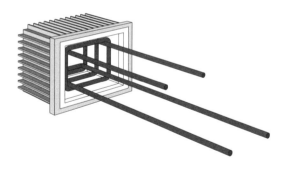

Fig. 72: Isokorb with connecting reinforcement

construction heights of the standard floors to be matched. Decoupling by means of supporting brackets can be useful for half-landings. > Figs. 71 and 72 A different finish can then be used for the landing.

In conclusion

On account of its enormous diversity and the constant improvements that have been made in the course of past decades, concrete remains one of the most important materials in the building industry. It consists of a number of different elements, which can be used as factors in determining and defining its performance. Whether the different kinds of reinforcement materials, the additives or concreting processes, the range allows concrete to be used in many different areas, from large bridge structures to furniture and property.

New mixes, reinforcement materials and techniques allow us to hope for advances in making concrete economical, sustainable and consequently forward-looking. Therefore, on both the design and construction levels, new opportunities and ways of using it will present themselves repeatedly in the future.

Appendix

STANDARDS AND GUIDELINES

DIN EN 197-1, Cement

DIN EN 206, Concrete - Specification, performance, production and conformity

DIN EN 934-2, Admixtures for concrete, mortar and grout

DIN EN 1008, Mixing water for concrete – Specification for sampling, testing and assessing the suitability of water, including water recovered from processes in the concrete industry, as mixing water for concrete

DIN EN 1504, Products and systems for the protection and repair of concrete structures – Definition, requirements, quality monitoring and evaluation of conformity

DIN EN 1520, Prefabricated reinforced components of lightweight aggregate concrete with open structure with structural or non-structural reinforcement

DIN EN 1990, Eurocode: Basis of structural design

DIN EN 1991, Eurocode 1: Impacts on structures

DIN EN 1992, Eurocode 2: Design of concrete structures

DIN EN 1994, Eurocode 4: Design of composite steel and concrete structures

DIN EN 1998, Eurocode 8: Design of structures for earthquake resistance

DIN EN 10138, Prestressing steels

DIN EN 12350, Testing fresh concrete

DIN EN 12354, Building acoustics – Estimation of acoustic performance of buildings from the performance of products

DIN EN 12390, Testing hardened concrete

DIN EN 12620, Aggregates for concrete

DIN EN 12812, Falsework – Performance requirements and general design

DIN EN 12878, Pigments for the colouring of building materials based on cement and/or lime – Specifications and methods of testing

DIN EN 13055-1, Lightweight aggregates

DIN EN 13225, Precast concrete elements – Linear structural elements

DIN EN 13369, General rules for precast concrete product

DIN EN 13501, Fire classification of construction products and building elements (the classifications according to DIN 4102 cannot be directly applied to the European 13501-1)

DIN EN 13670, Execution of concrete structures

DIN EN 14487, Sprayed concrete

DIN EN 14843, Precast concrete products – stairs

DIN EN 14889, Fibres for concrete

DIN EN 15037, Precast concrete products – Beam-and-block floor systems

ISO 21930, Sustainability in building construction – Environmental declaration of building products

ISO 21931, Susainability in building construction – Framework for methods of assessment of the environmental performance of construction works

ISO 15686, Buildings and constructed assets - Service life planning

LITERATURE

Edward Allen: *Fundamentals of Building Construction: Materials and Methods,* 6th edition, Hoboken, Wiley, New Jersey 2014

Andrea Deplazes (ed.): *Constructing Architecture*, Birkhäuser, Basel 2013

Kim S. Elliott: *Precast Concrete Structures,* Butterworth-Heinemann, Oxford, Boston, MA 2002

Awad S. Hanna: *Concrete Formwork Systems.* Civil and Environmental Engineering Series 2, Marcel Dekker, New York 1999

Manfred Hegger: *Basics Materials,* Birkhäuser, Basel 2007

Friedbert Kind-Barkauskas (ed.): *Concrete Construction Manual,* Birkhäuser; Edition Detail, Basel 2002

Alfred Meistermann: *Basics Loadbearing Systems,* Birkhäuser, Basel 2007

Martin Peck (ed.): *Modern Concrete Construction Manual: Structural Design, Material Properties, Sustainability,* Edition Detail. Munich: Institut für internationale Architektur-Dokumentation, Munich 2014

David Phillips and Megumi Yamashita: *Detail in Contemporary Concrete Architecture,* Laurence King Publishing, London 2012

PICTURE CREDITS

Figures 11, 14, 15: from the lecture notes for the subject building construction and design at Siegen University

Figure 31: Works by first-semester students, building construction and design, Siegen University

Figures 1, 2, 8, 13, 17 (part), 18, 20, 21, 24, 26, 39, 45:
Prof. Dr.-Ing. Bert Bielefeld

All other figures: Katrin Hanses

THE AUTHOR

Katrin Hanses, M.A. architect, is a research associate in the department of building construction and design at Siegen University and runs her own architecture practice in Cologne.

Series editor: Bert Bielefeld
Concept: Bert Bielefeld, Annette Gref

Translation from German into English:
James Roderick O'Donovan
English copy editing: Monica Buckland
Project management: Petra Schmid
Layout, cover design and typography:
Andreas Hidber
Typesetting and production: Amelie Solbrig

Library of Congress Cataloging-in-Publication
data
A CIP catalog record for this book has been
applied for at the Library of Congress.

Bibliographic information published by the
German National Library
The German National Library lists this publication in the Deutsche Nationalbibliografie;
detailed bibliographic data are available on
the Internet at http://dnb.dnb.de.

This publication is also available in a German
language edition (ISBN 978-3-0356-0361-3).

© 2015 Birkhäuser Verlag GmbH, Basel
P.O. Box 44, 4009 Basel, Switzerland
Part of Walter de Gruyter GmbH, Berlin/Boston

Printed on acid-free paper produced from
chlorine-free pulp. TCF ∞

Printed in Germany

ISBN 978-3-0356-0362-0

9 8 7 6 5 4 3 2 1

www.birkhauser.com